# Focus: The

*How to Use the Power of Focus to Live a Successful Life*

*By*

# *Vicki Joy*

## Other Books by Vicki Joy

ACNE: Natural Acne Scar Treatments for Clear Skin
http://amzn.to/29WlzA4

ANTI-AGING: The Anti-Aging Guide to Healthy Skin and the Fountain of Youth
http://amzn.to/1Q1P5CU

ANXIETY: Getting Free From Fear And Panic Attacks
http://amzn.to/1Thj2uS

ARTHRITIS: How to Relieve and Reverse Rheumatoid Arthritis Today
http://amzn.to/2a8bmLf

ASTHMA: How To Get Asthma Free Naturally
http://amzn.to/1Q8f6kj

FOCUS: The Key to Success
http://amzn.to/1rQsGoH

INTROVERT: How To Use The Introvert Advantage And Introvert Power
http://amzn.to/1XV8WH9

RELAXATION
http://amzn.to/1TTY6JM

WEIGHT LOSS - The Mindfulness Diet
http://amzn.to/1V6XMN7

UNSTOPPABLE YOU! How to Build Your Confidence
and Go After the Life of Your Dreams
http://amzn.to/2hhpwSw

**Copyright 2016 by author David James - All rights reserved.**

This document is geared towards providing exact and reliable information in regards to the topic and issue covered. The publication is sold with the idea that the publisher is not required to render accounting, officially permitted, or otherwise, qualified services. If advice is necessary, legal or professional, a practiced individual in the profession should be ordered.

*- From a Declaration of Principles which was accepted and approved equally by a Committee of the American Bar Association and a Committee of Publishers and Associations.*

In no way is it legal to reproduce, duplicate, or transmit any part of this document in either electronic means or in printed format. Recording of this publication is strictly prohibited and any storage of this document is not allowed unless with written permission from the publisher. All rights reserved.

The information provided herein is stated to be truthful and consistent, in that any liability, in terms of inattention or otherwise, by any usage or abuse of any policies, processes, or directions contained within is the solitary and utter responsibility of the recipient reader. Under no circumstances will any legal responsibility or blame be held against the publisher for any reparation, damages, or monetary loss due to the information herein, either directly or indirectly.

Respective authors own all copyrights not held by the publisher.

The information herein is offered for informational purposes solely, and is universal as so. The presentation of the information is without contract or any type of guarantee assurance.

The trademarks that are used are without any consent, and the publication of the trademark is without permission or backing by the trademark owner. All trademarks and brands within this book are for clarifying purposes only and are the owned by the owners themselves, not affiliated with this document.

# TABLE OF CONTENTS

Introduction

Chapter 1: Focus on Your Own Priorities

Chapter 2: Define Success on your Own Terms

Chapter 3: Choose to Have the Right Attitude

Chapter 4: Declutter Your Brain

Chapter 5: Be Consistent

Chapter 6: Visualize Success to Manifest It

Conclusion

# Introduction

Thank you and congratulations for purchasing this book, *"Focus - The Key to Success: How to Use the Power of Focus to Live a Successful Life."*

This book contains practical techniques and strategies on how to use the power of focus so that you can work towards building the life of your dreams. Everyone wants to live their dream life, but few of us actually go for it. We tend to get bogged down with the realities and responsibilities of everyday life, and our dreams seem to get further and further away from us. How do we reclaim our dreams? How can we actively pursue them? What will it take for us to actually live the lives we envisioned for ourselves? This book shares steps and ideas about how to be successful - how to stay on track in the pursuit of our dreams, and accomplish our goals.

You see, the secret to success - to accomplishing your goals and living your dreams - lies in the *power of focus*. Once you learn how to focus on the most important goals in your life, it becomes much easier to develop the strategies and the skills needed to accomplish them, and to see them become a reality.

In this book, we will discuss: the idea of success; setting clear goals; why focus is important; setting priorities; techniques for improving our ability to focus; and the importance of taking action in the direction of our dreams. Each chapter opens up with a famous quote that offers a dose of inspiration, and includes a story to help illustrate the principles being discussed. Thanks again and I hope you enjoy this book!

# Chapter 1 – Focus on Your Own
## Priorities

*"The key is not to prioritize what's on your schedule, but to schedule your priorities."*
*– Stephen Covey*

*Painting is Gabrielle's one true passion. Nothing makes her happier than sitting in front of an easel and canvas with a palette in one hand and a paintbrush in the other. Unfortunately, it has been years since Gabrielle last painted. That's because she has been dedicating all of her time and energy to her career, and to taking care of her family. You see, Gabrielle is the single mother and sole provider of two school aged children. Providing for herself and her children has become Gabrielle's top priority. As much as she loves to paint, she now thinks that indulging in her true passion is fruitless - painting won't help her pay off the mortgage, or pay her kids' tuition. Gabrielle often dreams of finding the time to paint, in spite of the daily demands at work. She still views painting is an important part of her life, but just has no time for it. By the end of the workday, she simply feels too exhausted to pick up a paintbrush.*

Does this sound familiar? Are there things in your life that you would love to accomplish, or even master, but you can't seem to find to time to pursue them? At this rate, Gabrielle's passion for her art will soon on go down the drain if she does not make pursuing it an important part of her life. While there is certainly nothing wrong with focusing on work obligations and family life, it is equally importantly to include time for personal well-being and personal growth as well.

How can Gabrielle find the time to pursue her passion for painting, and still manage to balance it out with the other seemingly more urgent aspects of her life? The answer is found in our ability to *focus*. As reported by CNBC, "according to Warren Buffett and Bill Gates, focus is the most important factor to success. Both men agree that relentlessly focusing on one specific passion or problem leads to achievement."

Focus can be described as the ability to concentrate; to bring something into the center of attention. Focus also refers to mental capacity. I like Pastor A.R. Bernard's definition of focus. He describes focus as: "bringing your mind, will, and emotions into alignment for what you have to do". This definition brings to mind a total commitment to reaching a particular target; to accomplishing our goals. He goes on to define focus as:

- A sensation of clarity and alertness (seeing things clearly, understanding things quickly);
- Fearlessness in the face of opposition (not being afraid of the challenges and obstacles between the dream and its manifestation);
- Confidence that you can do whatever you set your mind to;
- Keeping your head up, your eyes on the ball, and knocking the ball out the park (walking in dignity with your head held high as you overcome the obstacles on the way to your dreams and goals);
- Getting in the zone, staying on your toes, staying on target, staying on top of things

(focus is the antidote to laziness - you cannot be lazy if you are focused);

- Power ( focus empowers and energizes); and
- Taking hold of life and not letting go until your dreams become reality.

    *- Pastor A.R. Bernard (Christian Cultural Center)*

Focus is the ability to bring one's attention to bear - to 'zero in' - on a particular target. Targets here refer to dreams and goals. Focus is best expressed or understood in relation to goals, because it needs something to attach itself to. Goals are our targets - they are the things we wish to 'hit' or accomplish by a certain time. Our dreams and goals are the targets that focus attaches itself to. This is why is it so important to set clear goals. Get clear about what you want to accomplish. Know what you are going after. Focus is important because it serves as a bridge between our dreams and seeing our dreams come true. Focus makes us more efficient 'goal-getters'. Focus makes it much easier to accomplish a lot more goals in a given period of time.

Below are three useful strategies that we can implement to help us remain focused so that we can better manage the competing interests in our lives:

## 1. Manage Your Supply of Focus Wisely

We mentioned earlier that focus has to do with our mental capacity, and there is a limit on how much we can deal with mentally in a given day. Our ability to focus is at its maximum level the moment we wake up in the morning – that is when we are most alert. However, as the day wears on, our ability to focus begins to wane as we get inundated with different tasks (e.g., work obligations, interpersonal relationships etc.) that require our attention.

You can compare your ability to focus to the battery of your smartphone. Let's say you charge your phone overnight while you sleep. The moment you start using your phone again, the battery starts to become depleted. The more apps you use on your phone, the faster the battery will be depleted. Likewise, whenever we go to sleep or rest, we are 'charging' our mind and body. The moment we wake up and get busy about our day, our ability to focus, to fully concentrate on accomplishing all the things we need to get done, or would like to get done in a day, begin to be depleted.

Time and energy are essential elements in our ability to focus. The more time and energy we have, the greater our ability to focus. The less time and energy we have, the harder it becomes to focus. As such, our ability to focus is affected by the drain on our time and energy. Constantly remind yourself that you only have a limited supply of focus (i.e., time and energy to concentrate) each day. How you manage this supply is entirely up to you. Ideally, you should dedicate your time and energy to tackling the most urgent and important tasks at the start of your day, when your focus is sharpest. Unfortunately, this is often easier said than done.

Gabrielle, for example, spends the vast majority of her 'supply of focus' on her job. She ends up being incapable of pursuing her own passions after work because her focus supply is being rapidly depleted during her work day. By the time she gets home after work and takes care of her family, she no longer has the energy or enthusiasm for painting - or anything else for that matter. Gabrielle gets frustrated with herself for being 'too lazy' to get back into painting the way she would like to. However, what Gabrielle doesn't realize is that it's not about her being 'lazy'; but in fact, that her *mental capacity* has already been spent for the day.

Many of us can identify with Gabrielle's sense of frustration. We are often too 'spent' by the end of the day to do much else than crash on the couch. All our good intentions of maybe getting in some exercise; or catching up on some personal projects; or even spending quality time with family and friends, fall by the wayside. We are simply too exhausted – mentally and physically 'drained'– for anything more than grabbing a quick bite to eat and then falling to sleep.

## 2. Separate the Urgent from the Important

We tend to focus on the tasks we place the highest priority on. I like to think of priority as the level of urgency and/or importance. Priority levels (high priority, medium priority, low priority) are typically determined based on the consequences for leaving a task undone. The more dire the consequences for not completing a task, the higher the priority level assigned to that task. The assigned priority level determines where we place tasks on our list of things to do in a day. We consider urgent tasks as high priority; important tasks as medium priority; and tasks that are neither urgent nor particularly important (all other tasks) as low priority.

Simply put, the urgent tasks in your day are the ones that demand your immediate attention. These are the 'fires' that we have to 'put-out'. Important tasks on the other hand, while they also require our attention, are not as 'demanding' as urgent tasks - they don't have to be done immediately. Important tasks tend to be those tasks that carry more value and meaning to us, and are more in line with our personal goals. Another way to think about it is that high priority tasks (urgent tasks) are the *'have to do'* tasks; whereas medium-priority tasks (important tasks) have more of a *'should do'* element to them; and low-priority tasks (neither urgent nor important tasks) are those things we *'would like to do'*.

There are some tasks that are both urgent and important – they require immediate attention, and their accomplishment is valuable and meaningful to us. In many cases however, tasks are one or the other – urgent or important. Our issue here is that we tend to equate urgency with importance, which is not usually the case. The tasks we consider urgent (e.g., meeting a deadline at work) get top billing in our busy schedules, leaving little time or energy for the important tasks (e.g., taking care of our health), and other low-priority tasks.

In Gabrielle's case, her 'urgent tasks' are those related to her career. She needs to get them done first in order to keep her job, and thus, the means of financial support for herself and her children. This is the case with most of us, as our jobs are often our sole (or primary) source of income. As such, job responsibilities are considered high priority, and are at the top of our list of things to do in a given day. However, our urgent job-related tasks are often not in line with our personal goals. In fact, they are mostly in line with other people's goals (i.e., our boss, or the company we work for).

Important tasks - those 'should do' items - on the other hand, are usually much more in line with our own personal goals. Sadly, these tasks often get put on the back burner because they do not have glaring deadlines attached to them, unlike the urgent tasks. Also, by the time we get through with the urgent tasks - putting out the fires - we have little time or energy left for the important 'should do' tasks, or for the other low priority 'would like to do' tasks.

To find the time each day for the important things (i.e., exercise, recreational activities, quiet time, quality time with family etc.), we must first acknowledge them as important - as things that are meaningful and of value to us - as things that should be done.

One great technique for making room for important tasks/things is to create a modified to-do list. This list should be created at the end of each day in preparation for the following day. The first step is to write down the things you need to get done the next day, including the ones you deem as important and in line with your personal goals. Gabrielle's to-do list might look something like this:

- finish the end-of-month report for work,
- paint my self-portrait,
- buy groceries, and
- prepare a slow-cooked dinner.

Next, grab a red pen and write a big red "I" next to the tasks that are important to you. Remember, the important tasks are those in line with your personal or family goals. Going back to Gabrielle's to-do list, she would  mark "I" next to "paint my self-portrait." After distinguishing the important tasks from the urgent ones, you can make time to work on the important ones  first thing in the morning - before your day gets hijacked by all the urgent tasks.

### 3. Begin Each Day with Your Most Important Tasks

After identifying the important tasks, make sure to start the day working on the most important one of them, if at all possible.  This might mean waking up a bit earlier to carve out enough time in your morning to take care of the one task/thing from your list of important tasks that you have identified as most important in moving you toward your personal goals. If waking up earlier is not doable for you, you might consider re-purposing how you spend those first waking moments before you have to head out the door to face another busy day. Maybe you reach for an electronic device in the morning to browse personal email, texts or social media. Maybe you like to sit down to a leisurely breakfast while watching the morning news. Maybe you spend awhile just going through your closet trying to figure out what to wear, and preparing a bag lunch to take to work with you.

I always used to complain about not having enough time until I figured out I could *find time'* by addressing some of my time wasters. Making some simple tweaks to my old morning habits opened up some much needed time for me to tackle the most important tasks on my to-do list first thing in the day. Instead of reaching for my smartphone first thing in the morning, I delayed 'checking-in' with social media for my commute time (if I was not driving in to work), or for during my lunch break at work. Instead of sitting down to breakfast in front of the TV, I make a nutritious smoothie to have on the go, and catch up on the day's top headlines on a newsfeed on my smartphone. I pick out my work outfits and prepare my bag lunch the night before, thus significantly freeing up some time in my mornings to work on some important personal goals (important tasks).

With these few tweaks, I didn't need to wake up any earlier, but easily 'found' an 'extra' forty-five minutes in the morning before I head off to work. One of my important personal goals is improved health and well-being. I use this 'extra' time in the morning for prayer and meditation, and for exercise. By making the time to get this done first thing in the mornings, I have in essence given an important task (working on my meaningful personal goals) top priority, over the urgent tasks that await me at the office.

It is essential to begin the day by working on your important tasks - those tasks that are in line with your personal goals. The late Jim Rohn, master motivational speaker and my all-time favorite personal development teacher, emphasized *"Work harder on yourself than you do on your job"*. That is the idea here. ***Use your best energy and sharpest focus to work on your own goals!*** Take care of your own goals before you head out to take care of someone else' (your boss' or your company's goals). After putting out fires all day, and working on urgent but often unimportant tasks, your focus (time and energy) will usually be too depleted by the end of the day to work on your own goals. Make yourself your top priority!

# Chapter 2 – Define Success on your Own Terms

*"The biggest adventure you can ever take is to live the life of your dreams."*
*– Oprah Winfrey*

*Ever since he was little, Corey knew that he was born to tell stories. In fact, he wants to write a science fiction novel and he's been working on it, albeit on and off, for years. After college, he took a part-time job at a coffee shop so that he could spend more time working on his novel. However, he soon notices that his friends and former classmates have been enrolling in graduate programs. Most of them were pursuing careers as doctors, lawyers, or engineers. His own parents are even pressuring him to pursue a more 'traditional' career because they feel that he's wasting his potential chasing after his 'pipe-dream' of becoming a writer. It isn't long before Corey begins to feel unaccomplished, and starts to lose his focus on his dream to become an author. Should he abandon his dream of becoming a writer and pursue a more conventional path towards 'success?'*

Corey's dilemma is certainly not uncommon. Society (including family and friends) has its own way of defining 'success', even though this cookie cutter definition may not be right for everyone. That is why it is important for each of us to know and value our own talents, and to nurture our own dreams. You should never say that you are "just" a writer, or "just" an artist, or "just" anything. Adding "just" to your dream occupation diminishes it. It suggests that your dream, or talent, or particular skill-set is not quite good enough, and therefore does not quite measure up to society's definition of success. *Your definition of success is the only definition that truly matters!*

It's easy to focus on pursuing those goals and dreams that conform with society's definition of success. It becomes much more difficult to remain focused on our dreams, however, when we decide to go against the grain, to march to the beat of our own drum, to go after the desires of our heart. Often times our family and friends - those closest to us - don't understand or support our pursuit of our dreams. This is why it is so crucial to be your own cheerleader. You will need to be able to encourage yourself in order to remain focused on your goals in the face of opposition.

Here are a couple of tips on how to keep your focus on your goals and dreams, especially when they don't line up with others' expectations, or with others' definition of success:

## 1. Stop Comparing Yourself to Others

I came across a quote that stuck with me, and it goes something like this - *"stop comparing your beginning with someone else's middle"*. In our pursuit of our goals and dreams, we sometimes get discouraged when we notice how much farther along the path to 'success' others seem to be when compared to us. This quote reminds me that we are all unique, with our own distinct set of goals and dreams that we would love to see manifest in our lives. As such, my vision for my life will be quite different than my friend's vision for his life. Your idea of what success looks like to you will be quite different from your peers' definition of success.

We are all at different points or stages of our journeys toward 'success'. While I am now starting to actively work on my dream for my life, my friend might have been steadily plugging away at his dream for years. It would be unreasonable for me to expect the same level of results at the beginning of my journey as the results or outcomes my friend is experiencing well into his journey. Even if we both started out working on our dreams at the same time, our results will vary simply because our dreams and goals vary. Comparing our level of 'success' with others' is an exercise in futility, simply because we are working toward different goals. The saying that 'the grass is greener on the other side' is not necessarily true. The grass on my side can be just as green if I focus on keeping it well watered.

The objective here is to resist the temptation to compare ourselves with others. To achieve this aim, get so busy working on your own goals and dreams, that you don't have the time or inclination to notice or compare yourself with others' progress.

There is more than enough 'success' to go around. Hang in there; keep plugging away at your own goals; keep working on your own dreams; wish your peers well on their journey; knowing that each of us will 'get there' once we stay focused on our own 'grass'.

Another big reason why you should stop comparing yourself to others is that you are making _them_ your focus, instead of making _you_ your focus. As you know, this is a waste of valuable time and energy that would be much better used to concentrate on hitting our own targets, on accomplishing our own goals. Comparing ourselves to others yields absolutely no benefit to us. Rather, this kind of comparison may leave us feeling 'less than' - like we are not quite measuring up. Comparison also assumes that we are all running the same race, or on the same journey, and therefore can be measured by the same thresholds or milestones.

I am a huge fan of all things 'personal development' and of inspirational and motivational quotes in particular. These little nuggets help keep me track when I am otherwise tempted to lose sight of my dreams. The motivational quotes below have been very useful in helping me keep my eyes focused on my own dreams and goals, and not compare myself to others:

*"I am not interested in competing with anyone. I hope we all make it."*

*– Erica Cook*

*"A flower does not think of competing with the flower next to it. It just blooms."*

*– Zenkei Shibayama*

*"I am in competition with no one. I have no desire to play the game of being better than anyone. I am simply trying to be better than I was yesterday." – Unknown*

## 2. Eliminate (Future) Regrets

Another tip for staying focused on your goals and dreams is to imagine that you are trying to eliminate the possibility of future regrets. Imagine that you have reached a ripe old age and are about to write your memoir, or share your life story with your great grandchildren. You would happily share all the highlights of your life - the loves, the accomplishments, the special occasions. But what about the regrets? What would be those things, those dreams, those goals, that looking back you wished you had accomplished, you wished you had pursued. These are what I mean by 'future' regrets. It's all those things that you would do if you had the chance to do it all over again.

Visualize the kind of success you want to have before you die. Do you wish you spent more time with your family and friends? Do you wish you were able to written the novel you have been dreaming of writing for years? Do you wish you had gone on to graduate school when you had the chance? Do you wish you had practiced healthy habits and lost the excess weight so that you could have enjoyed a more, vibrant, active, confident lifestyle? Do you wish that you had learned French so that you could have retired to France? Do you wish you had the confidence to say hello to that person that made your heart sing when you had the opportunity to? This list can endless, but it does not need to be, because we can start right now, in this moment, to begin to move our lives in the direction of our dreams.

Whatever 'regrets' you came up with during this exercise, write them down. Now, use this list of 'regrets' to shape your own version of success. *Turn this list of regrets into your list of goals!* You can then focus on achieving these goals to eliminate any future regrets. Now, when the time actually comes for you to tell your life's story - to write your memoir - you can tell the story with satisfaction of a life  well lived, of dreams fulfilled.  Only you can know what a life well lived means to you, and often all that's needed is the focus and the courage to go for it.

# Chapter 3 – Choose to Have the Right Attitude

*"Your attitude, not your aptitude, will determine your altitude."*
*– Zig Ziglar*

Tiffani's lifelong dream is to travel the world. The problem though, is that she feels as though life always gets in her way. For instance, she is overwhelmed at work, and can't take time off for a hard earned and much needed vacation. To make matters worse, her boss behaves like a tyrant, and keeps giving Tiffani more and more assignments that are way outside her job scope. Tiffani hates it, but feels stuck in her job. The economy is sluggish and she feels that she won't be able to find another job with a comparable salary if she quits this one - and she can't afford to be without a salary. This seemingly intolerable situation is making Tiffani resent her boss and dread the very thought of going to the office.

To add insult to injury, Tiffani sees all the photos her friends post online from their *travel around the world, and longs to be traveling with them also. What happened? How did she get here? She was supposed to be on her second passport by now. This is not how her life was supposed to go. Tiffani feels frustrated by being 'trapped' in her life.*

Sadly, many of us can identify with Tiffani's attitude toward her job in particular, and toward her life in general. After all, it is all too easy to just blame our frustrations on external factors. We are all too quick to blame the boss, our partner, our parents, the bills, or our friends for holding us back in life. However, the truth of the matter is that we are solely responsible for our own lives. The responsibility for where we find ourselves in life lies squarely on our own shoulders. *We are where we are at any given stage in live because of the choices we have made!* That may be a bitter pill to swallow depending our circumstances, but unless and until we accept that hard truth, we will continue to feel frustrated and 'stuck'.

*"Life is 10% percent what happens to you, and 90% how you respond to it."*
*– Charles R. Swindoll*

Not only are we solely responsible for where we are in life, we are also solely responsible for our attitude toward the circumstances in our lives. By not taking responsibility of your own attitude, you are allowing the rest of the world to dictate how you should think and feel each day; thereby allowing external factors to push you around, and cause you to lose focus on your own goals and your own priorities.

However, the good news is that we have the ability at any moment to overcome our negative attitudes and unleash our full potential. It all lies in the power of choice. In other words, we can *choose* to be responsible for our own actions and reactions. We get to choose how we see the world. We get to choose how we see the possibilities for our lives. We get to choose how we earn our living. We get to choose who we surround ourselves with. We get to choose the life we want to life. It really is quite simple, although it does take some courage. Make the conscious effort to end the habit of blaming others, to stop believing that you are simply the victim of chance. Adopt the right attitude - the attitude that says *"I am responsible for my own life, and I can start right now to build the life of my dreams!"*.

Below are two useful strategies to help us hone the right attitude and take responsibility for our own lives:

## 1. Respond, Don't Just React

When life dishes out a challenge, it seems like our default setting is to react in a negative way. However, we can control our reactions; and by so doing, control our lives. When faced with a difficult situation, first take a step back and think about the best way to *respond* to the situation. I like to think of this as 'practicing the pause'. Take a moment to take a deep breath and gather your thoughts, or whisper a prayer, before responding to the situation. Do this often enough, and you will begin to retrain the mind to respond instead of react. The pause gives you time and space to consider the wisest course of action regarding any given situation.

## 2. Self-Reflection

Self-reflection, or self-evaluation, is a powerful habit for helping to develop a right - a positive - attitude. It allows us to assess who we are, where were are, and where we would like to go in life. This self-evaluation exercise pushes us to get clear about our goals, and puts the onus on us for their accomplishment. It is a priceless tool for helping us to refocus on our goals and for moving us in the direction of our dreams.

There are several methods for self-reflection, but one of the easiest and most effective ways is to keep a journal. Write down your thoughts, and then read them again afterwards or the next day. This little habit holds tremendous power that will allow you to gain clarity, to develop a more positive attitude, and to make even better decisions - decisions that move you in the direction of your goals and dreams.

In the example of Tiffani above, adopting the right attitude might help her to realize that she is not as 'stuck' as she might think. Instead of complaining about all the 'out of scope' assignments her boss gives her, Tiffani might view this as the valuable expansion of her skills set. With these new skills, Tiffani begins to notice better job opportunities for herself, even in a sluggish economy. Now, instead of reacting with resentment toward her boss, Tiffani chooses to respond with gratitude for the opportunity to learn and to enhance her curriculum vitae. With this newfound sense of confidence in her professional growth, Tiffani starts sending out applications for her dream job. So while her boss did not change, or her job change, *Tiffani changed because her attitude changed*. By adopting this new winning attitude and focusing on the things that are important to her, in no time Tiffani lands her dream job, and changes her life!

Adopting the right attitude has been one of the best things that I have done for myself. It took a whole of pressure and stress off of me, and made my life a lot more enjoyable. I decided to let go of the 'victim mentality' and choose to take full responsibility for my reactions to the events of my life. I choose to optimistic. I choose to see the best in each situation. I choose to see the good in others. I choose to believe that life is good and that people are kind. I have been called naive and 'sheltered' in the process, but that is quite okay. Because, adopting this positive attitude toward life has empowered me to go after my dreams.

This positive outlook on life has allowed me to expect the very best that life has to offer, and to expect to see my dreams come true. Instead of complaining when things did not seem to be going my way, I chose to view it as an opportunity to grow, or to change. Adopting a right - a positive - attitude allows me move through life with a confident expectation of good. This shift in attitude has allowed me to fearlessly pursue my dreams. It has help me become courageous enough to walk away from a decades long career to pursue my dream of become an author and an entrepreneur. Zig Ziglar had it right - our attitude determines our altitude.

# Chapter 4 – Declutter Your Brain

*It does not take much strength to do things, but it requires a great deal of strength to decide what to do."*
*– Elbert Hubbard*

*Jason has become known as the 'go-to man.' If his friends, family, or colleagues need help with anything, they know they can just go to Jason. While everyone likes Jason, he himself constantly feels overwhelmed by the amount of decisions he has to make in a day. He feels like he is being pulled in all different directions; however, Jason simply cannot say "no" when called upon for help. He is so involved in taking care of everyone's issues (making decisions for them), that he finds it difficult to focus on his own goals and tasks. By the end of the day, Jason's 'supply of focus' is depleted from sorting out other people's problems. While his dedication to serving and helping others is quite admirable, all of the resulting commitments leave him with little to no time or energy (essential elements that impact our ability to focus) to work on his own goals and dreams.*

*All the decisions that Jason is making during the course of the day are for the benefit of others (solving their problems, making their lives easier), and do very little to help move him in the direction of his own dreams. How can he find the balance between his desire to help others, and focusing on his own goals? How can he decide which things to say yes to, and which things to take a pass on? How can be become a more effective decision-maker, so that he can free up some valuable time and energy (mental capacity) to work on his own dreams?*

Jason is certainly not alone in his predicament. We are all faced with tons of choices each day. However, to 'find' the time work on our important task - those that are more in line with our personal goals - we must master the art of decision making. *We must learn to declutter our brains to improve our mental capacity.* We must learn to take on fewer 'mental tasks' in a given day. We must learn to be more decisive. In many cases, our inability to make a decision is directly linked to our fear of saying "no". We worry about hurting others' feelings if we say "no" to a request they make of us. We worry about losing friendships, or about making things feel awkward, if we say "no" to our friends, family, or colleagues. What if they don't like me anymore if I say "no"? What if they think I am not a nice person if I say "no"? What if they talk badly about me if I am no longer the 'yes-man' they know me to be? Our fear of saying "no" stems from our need to please, our desire to be well-liked and well-thought of. While all noble aspirations, this 'disease to please' can be quite destructive if it comes at the expense of our own well-being.

The truth of the matter is that the people in our lives that truly care about us will understand that we simply cannot meet all their needs. They will understand that there are times when we simply cannot 'be there' for them at the drop of a dime. They will understand that we have our own lives, and our own issues, and our own priorities that require our focus (our time and attention). They will understand that we simply cannot accommodate their every demand on our time and energy. Or, we would hope that they would understand. But even if they don't understand, that is okay also. In time they will come around. Or they might not. Regardless, we must have (or develop) the courage to say "no". Saying "no" does not mean that you are being selfish or uncaring. It simply means that you need to say "yes" to yourself; that you have chosen to give your goals and tasks priority; that your well-being is more important than others' perception of you. In saying "no" to all the external drains on our time and energy, we are saying "yes" to focusing on our goal, and to pursuing the life of our dreams. *Sometimes saying "no" to others is the best "yes" we can give to ourselves!*

Below are a couple strategies to help declutter our brains, and free up some valuable mental capacity to focus on your own goals and dreams:

## 1. Make Fewer Choices

In Chapter 1 we talked about the concept of focus as something that is of limited supply. This becomes more apparent whenever you make decisions each day. I like the Google definition of a decision as "a conclusion or resolution reached after consideration." The *process* and *action* of 'consideration' requires mental energy. The more decisions that we are confronted with in a day, the more mental energy we are expending. The more mental energy we use up in a day, the less we have available to focus on our important tasks and goals.

A good technique for retaining high levels of focus for important tasks is to reduce the number of decisions you make every day. Consider how you go about each day. For at least one day, monitor the number of decisions you had to make. Keep a little notebook with you or record it on your smartphone. From the time you wake up until the end of that day, be mindful of the choices you had to make. What should you have for breakfast? Which outfit are you going to wear? Which route are you going to take to work? Where are you going to park? What are to going to have for lunch? What are you going to have for dinner? Which task at work will you tackle first? Which emails should you reply to? What should you say in your reply? And the list goes on and on.

At the end of the day, review your list of 'decisions'. Consider whether or not you can put any of these decisions on autopilot. For example, if choosing what to wear stresses you out at the start of each day that activity is already eating up a significant amount of your mental capacity - your focus supply. Unless this decision-making process is important to you, you can choose to put it on autopilot. You may adopt a capsule wardrobe. With a capsule wardrobe, you limit your clothing options to just a few key pieces that you can easily mix and match to always look presentable. Jennifer Scott from the Daily Connoisseur (http://dailyconnoisseur.blogspot.com) is an excellent resource for learning how to put together a capsule wardrobe. Or you may choose to adopt what I like to call the 'uniform approach'. This involves wearing the same or similar outfit each day. This approach was made famous by Facebook CEO Mark Zuckerberg who is known to wear the same type of grey T-shirt to work each day.

Maybe you spend a lot of time and energy figuring out what to make for dinner. This daily stressful process can be eliminated by a bit of advance meal prep. My cousin Cheryl has a great strategy for doing this. She sets aside one day a week to do all her cooking for the upcoming week. So on Sundays, she cooks several large pots of various dishes. She then parcels them out in individual portion sizes and freezes them. Come lunch time or dinner time, it just takes her a few minutes to reheat the dish and she has a delicious, nutritious, homemade meal at the ready.

In Jason's case, he can put a firm yet polite "no" response on autopilot. When he is being leaned on, and pulled by friends or family or colleagues, he can whip out his automatic "no" to keep himself from being drained by others. The trick is to decide ahead of time that you are limiting the added responsibilities that you are willing to take on in a given day, and have a few responses at the ready in anticipation of excessive demands on your valuable time and energy. Your bag of autopilot responses might sound something like this: "No, I won't be able to help you with that;" or, "No, I can't fit that into my schedule into my schedule today;" or "No, I don't get involved in those situations." You get the idea. Practice a few firm yet polite "no" responses that are appropriate for those requests that come your way that just drain you of the time and/or energy you need to focus on accomplishing your own goals.

## 2. Eliminate Potential Distractions

Another way to simplify the decision-making process is to eliminate distractions, or potential distractions. A distraction is basically any obstacle in the way of whatever we are focused on. These distractions often pop up during unexpected times and ruin our focus, despite our best intentions. One such distraction is the internet and social media. A recent report by www.digitaltrends.com estimated that we spend an average of four to five hours browsing on-line daily.

There are a couple techniques for eliminating the distraction of mindless internet browsing or channel surfing. The best and most effective way to eliminate these distractions is simply to turn off the electronic device. You can limit the amount of time you allot yourself each day for these activities, and then set a specific time for going off-line. I have a friend that allots one hour per day for what she calls her 'entertainment activities'. She spends one hour in the evenings watching television, and catching up on her social media feeds during the commercial breaks. Once the hour is up, she simply turns off the television and turns off her smartphone. For others, this 'cold turkey' approach might be too drastic. An alternative might be to set the timer on the television set to shut off after a certain amount of viewing time. To help limit the time spent mindlessly surfing the net, you might consider installing an online app that would block you from accessing your favorite time-wasting websites.

Another potential distraction comes in the form of our 'random thoughts.' There are certainly moments when you are trying to focus on a particular task, but suddenly find your mind wandering in all different directions. You find yourself thinking about everything else but the task at hand. And, the longer your mind wanders, the harder it seems to harness your thoughts and refocus on the task at hand. Even if these random thoughts are about important issues in our lives, they are still distractions if they do not contribute to the current task you are working on. When you find your mind wandering, you can simply take a moment to acknowledge the random thoughts, then set them aside and refocus on the task at hand. A simply way to set aside a random thought, is to replace it with another thought, or replace it with a statement. In this case, you would replace the random thoughts with thoughts about your priorities. Or, you might make a simple statement to refocus your attention like: "I am currently working on... and I am focusing on that." Just making an affirming statement will help to eliminate the other mental distractions.

Finally, to help eliminate distractions, you should make your workspace more conducive to maintaining your focus. Get rid of clutter. Organize your space. Keep it neat and clean. Only keep the items in your workspace that will motivate you to work on your priorities, or the tools needed to work on your goals. Make your space inviting and calming. Decorate it to your liking, with the aim that this will be your 'goal-getting' space.

Remove any items from your workspace that might tempt you to lose focus and waste time. You might consider removing any television sets or entertainment centers from this space. Establish a strict 'do not disturb' policy for the times that you are in your workspace focusing on your priorities and working on your goals. The objective is to declutter your workshop - free it from anything that might result in distractions or mental clutter.

# Chapter 5 – Be Consistent

*"Consistency is the key to every victory."*
*– Joyce Meyer*

*At the beginning of the year, Vicki was on a roll. She had made a commitment to lose the excess weight and get fit and healthy once and for all. She had enrolled at the local gym and had been working out for 45 minutes, five times per week. She had completely wiped her pantry clean of all junk food and stocked up on healthy, whole foods. She had even prepared plenty of low calorie, nutritious meals in advance, and frozen them, so that she would have healthy meals ready to quickly reheat for dinner.*

*Alas, after two weeks of intense focus on her weight lost goals, Vicki lost her motivation and ran out of steam. She had some muscle aches as a result of exercising for the first time in years. So, she used these aches as an excuse to skip the gym for a few days. During that time, she felt she had earned a break, so she went out to a buffet dinner with friends, and indulged in all her favorite rich dishes. It wasn't long before Vicki went right back to her old, sedentary lifestyle. She feels like a failure for yet again falling back into the old unhealthy patterns, and is on the verge of giving up on her goal of losing the weight and getting lean and fit, and feeling better.*

Many of us can identify with Vicki's story. We set goals - have a clear target - and then set off full steam ahead to accomplish them. The start of the journey is exciting. We are motivated and eager to get going. In my case, I set weight loss as my top New Year's resolution. I went out and bought new gym clothes, new sneakers, and even a new eco-friendly water bottle to take to the gym. I bought now glass storage containers and created meal plans so that I could prepare and store healthy meals in advance. I downloaded new playlists of up-tempo music to keep me pumped while I exercised. I was ready to finally win my life-long battle with weight. I was off to a great start. Sadly, I started skipping workouts, and then slowly fell back into my old unhealthy eating habits. Within a month, I had given up on my weight loss goals and just starting buying bigger clothes.

You see, long-term success requires consistency. The energy and excitement that are present at the beginning of any journey (any pursuit of a goal or a dream) often do not last long enough to see you through to the end of the journey. The ability to remain focused on our goals, and to consistently take actions that move us in the direction of our goals, are crucial elements in success.

I like to think of consistency as taking action on a regular basis. It is doing what should be done, regardless of our feelings, or changes in circumstances. It is about those routine, often mundane actions, that by themselves don't seem too significant; but taken over time, result in massive progress. It's the daily grind of taking the 30-minute walk; eating healthy balanced meals; drinking the recommended 8 cups of water daily; and getting adequate rest, that results in a transformed body by the end of the year - the amazing before and after photos.

My favorite songwriter Chris Rice has a lyric in the song 'Magic Wand' that says: *"The only way to really change is simple choice every day..."*. This sums up the importance of consistency in the accomplishment of our goals. It's the routine, everyday choices we make that will determine whether we stay on track toward our goals, or run out of steam and give up on our dreams. It is easy to lose sight on our goals in the routine of the daily grind.

The time between dreaming the dream and ultimately living the dream can seem long and tedious. This is the time between the 'before photo' and the 'after photo'. It is during this time that we are most tempted to lose focus and throw in the towel. It is during this time that we start to make excuses. It is during this time that can fall back into the old patterns that sabotage our success. It is during this time that we are most susceptible to distractions. However, it is during this time that our capacity to remain focused on our dreams is most needed. Our ability to keep our eyes firmly fixed on the target (or dreams, or goals) will pull us through the challenges of the daily grind and help us reach our goals.

To become truly successful - to reach our goals and live our dreams - we must remain consistent. We must do those mundane, routine, daily tasks that we would rather not have to do. Below are a couple of useful tips to help us keep your eyes on the prize and take consistent action in the direction of our dreams, no matter how long our journey to success may take:

## 1.  Be Mindful of your Reason

To maintain the ability to focus, constantly keep in mind the reason behind the goal. The reason why you believe something is important is actually your main source of motivation, and the driving force behind your power to focus. Whenever you lose focus, ask yourself this question: "Why do I want this?" Be clear and honest with your answer. Write your reasons down, and review them regularly to help you stay on track with doing the routine daily task necessary to accomplish your goals.

For instance, Vicki should remind herself of the reasons why she had the strong desire to lose weight and improve her lifestyle.  It may be that she was informed by her doctor about the dangers of her current health condition, and that she should do something about it. If that is her main reason, then she should use this as her reminder every time she considers skipping the gym or choosing junk food over healthy meals. It may be that she wants to have the energy to keep up with her child and engage in outdoor activities with her family. It might be that she just wants to feel good, and look good in the clothes that she would like to wear. It might be that she wants to age gracefully and enjoy a level of vitality in her senior years. Whatever her reasons, she would write them down and review them regularly to help her stay the course and remain consistent on her way to accomplishing her goals.

## 2. **Always Try Again - Never Give Up**

> *"Fall seven times, stand up eight."*
> *- Japanese Proverb*

Another tip for helping with consistency is that it is okay to mess up sometimes. It happens. Even with the best of intentions, there will be times that we fail, that we veer off course, that we fall down on our journey to accomplishing our goals. Making a mistake does not mean that we are doomed to fail. The key is to get right back up and back on course. Don't stay down, don't stay off course. So you did not go the gym every day this week like you hoped, and you did not stick to your meal plan for the week. Own it, let it go, and then move on. Pick yourself up, dust yourself off, and then get right back to doing the daily tasks necessary to reach your goals. *It is okay to fall down sometimes - just don't stay down!*

It is said that when an airplane takes off for a new destination, that airplane is off course 90% of the time. However, the airplane still manages to reach its intended destination. How can this be? How can an airplane be off course for the vast majority of the flight and still reach its intended destination? It does this by *continually correcting its course!* With consistent course correction, the airplane makes it to its destination. The same is true for us as we attempt to accomplish our goals and live life on our own terms. The key is to get right back on course whenever we veer off course. Course-correcting is easier than we might think. It requires an acceptance that we will fail somethings. Accepting that fact might be difficult because we don't like the idea of failing.

However, the quicker we accept that some level of failure - of missing the mark - is inevitable whenever we attempt to 'go for it', the quicker we can take the steps needed to get back on track. So when you fall down, you never have to stay down - you can always try again.

# Chapter 6 – Visualize Success to Manifest It

*"All successful men and women are big dreamers. They imagine what their future could be, ideal in every respect, and then they work every day toward their distant vision, that goal or purpose."*
*– Brian Tracy*

*Clintross feels like a robot. He wakes up at the same time each morning and goes through the same ritual each workday. He takes the same route each day to the same job that he has had for the past ten years, where his day is filled with a series of monotonous tasks. This job does not fulfil him, but it is a steady paycheck, and he has simply gotten used to it. Clintross used to dream of owning a business, but he's never really gotten around to actually starting it. He still thinks of making the leap to being an entrepreneur, but can't seem to drum up the motivation to get things going. He keeps telling himself that he'll get started soon, but 'soon' never seem to come. Clintross feels that he lacks the inspiration, the push, to really make his dream of becoming an entrepreneur a reality. He has tried reading personal development books and the success stories of other entrepreneurs, but none of these really got him past the daydreaming stage.*

What can Clintross do to get the boost of motivation he needs to get started on the path to making his dream of owning a business a reality? How can he get past the daydreaming stage, and start to take action in the direction of his dreams? A useful technique for jumpstarting the 'goal-getting' process, for fueling focus and drive, is visualization.

Visualization is the practice of 'seeing' the outcome you would like to have - of imagining your goals as if they were already accomplished. It's getting and holding a clear picture in your mind's eye of your desired future. When you have and hold a clear mental image of what you want to achieve, it becomes a lot more likely that you will achieve it.

Our imagination is a much more powerful tool than you give it credit for. Apart from enabling us to come up with creative solutions to the various issues we face in a given day, it can also help boost our self-confidence and help us focus on our goals. There is a wonderful account in the Bible of God's promise to Abraham to make him the father of many nations. This was a miraculous promise, because Abraham and his wife were not only childless at the time the promise was made, but they were also past child-bearing age. To help build Abraham's faith, to help him get an image of abundance, God guided Abraham through a 'visualization exercise'. To help Abraham 'see' the generations that would be born from him - the many nations - God got Abraham to get an image of the stars in the sky so that he could grasp the concept of a multitude.

> *And He brought him outside and said, "Look toward heaven, and number the stars, if you are able to number them." Then He said to him, "So shall your offspring be."*
>
> *- Genesis 15:5*

With visualization, you are imprinting a picture of your dreams, of your accomplished goals, on your brain. I like to think of it as taking mental snapshots of your goals, and reviewing and replaying these snapshots in your imagination on a regular basis. Through visualization, you are convincing your mind that what you want, what you desire, is not only possible, but that it is a reality for you.

Below are some useful tips on how to use visualization to help your reach your goals:

**1. Visualize Only When You Believe That It Works**

Visualization and belief go hand in hand. For visualization to work well, you must belief that it is a powerful tool for helping you to maintain your focus on your journey to success. If you are still skeptical of the concept, I recommend that you do some further research to learn more about the effectiveness of this technique.

Once you are willing to step into the process of visualization with an open mind and a genuine desire to see yourself achieve your goals, then is the ideal time to give it a try. Find a quiet place where you can spend some uninterrupted time. Think about the goals and dreams that you want see come to pass in your life. It might also be helpful to have actually photos that represent your dreams that can help you focus on your goals. Now picture yourself as already living your dream. Imagine yourself already having your desired outcome. Allow yourself to feel all the emotions that go along with having you dreams come through. If your dream is financial freedom, imagine yourself financially free. Where would you live? How would you dress? What type of car would you drive? How would you spend your days? What charities would you donate to? See yourself writing the donation checks to your favorite charities, and feel the joy of being able to help others and change lives. You get the idea. Do this for each of your goals. Imagine yourself with the outcomes that you desire, and feel the joy and gratitude of having accomplished your goals.

Jim Carrey, famous actor and comedian, told the story in a 1997 appearance on the Oprah Winfrey show of how he used the power of visualization to feel better, and to accomplish his dreams. As a struggling actor at the beginning of his career - when he had nothing - Jim Carrey would drive through Hollywood, and visualize himself as an actor that was in high demand. He imagined that top directors were seeking him out to star in their films. He took his visualization exercise a step further. He wrote out a check to himself for $10,000,000 (ten million dollars) for 'acting services rendered'. He post-dated the check for three years later, for right before Thanksgiving 1995. He kept this check in his wallet so that he would see it constantly over the years, and tells how the check began to deteriorate because of the length of time it was in his wallet. He went on to tell that he found out right before Thanksgiving 1995 that he was cast as a star in a movie, for which he would be paid ten million dollars.

In Clintross' case, he should first set some clear goals about what being an entrepreneur means to him. Then he can start to visualize himself living as if those goals were already accomplished. He could imagine himself signing multi-million dollar contracts for his business. He can imagine the employees he would hire. He could imagine a waiting list of clients clamoring for his services. In this visualization exercise, Clintross should be as detailed as possible - from the types of products he is manufacturing, to his company's name, mission and vision statements, and so on. He might also watch YouTube videos, listen to podcasts, and read books about other successful entrepreneurs who are doing what he would like to do.

> *"Whatever your mind can conceive and believe the mind can achieve regardless of how many times you may have failed in the past."*
> - *Napoleon Hill*

You too should spend as much time as you can painting the perfect picture of yourself as a success. The visualization exercise should make you feel good, and it should spark the desire in you to stay focused on your goals and go for your dreams!

## 2. Reverse Engineer your Vision of Success

During and right after the visualization exercise, you will notice your perspective changing - you will start to see and feel that your dreams and goals are achievable. You now have a much clearer image of yourself as a success, and can come up with different strategies on how to turn this vision into reality. This is where the 'reverse engineering' process will come into play. It is a lot like figuring out the best path through a maze, but you are starting in reverse, at the finish line, and working your way backwards.

To start reverse engineering your path to success, ask yourself this question after your visualization exercise: "How did I become such a success?" Imagine all the steps it would have taken for you to reach your goals. Then write down these steps and ideas. These notes will serve as your guide to determining what you should focus on.

The final and most important step is to believe in your vision of success. No matter how far away you currently are from your dreams, believe that they are possible for you. Some people like to use the phrase "fake it 'til you make it", and this concept has helped many people stay on track toward their goals. Clintross, for example, can take the next step in his visualization exercise by printing up business cards, and dressing like a businessman - even if he is still in the process of creating his business plan. He can start looking at potential office spaces. All these actions in the direction of his dreams will help cement his belief that his dreams can come true for him.

*"All things are possible to those who believe."*
                                            *- Mark 9:23*

Give visualization a try.  Let your imagination roam freely.  Allow yourself to see your goals and dreams as having come true.  Allow yourself to believe that whatever you are dreaming for your life is possible for you.  Allow yourself to feel deserving of those things that you desire for your life.  If you can see it in your mind, you can see it, eventually, in reality.   Allow yourself to be energized on your journey to success by the power of seeing you dreams as reality.

# Conclusion

*"The successful warrior is the average man with laser-like focus."*

- *Bruce Lee*

The ability to remain focused on our goals is a major key to success. Focus is an attribute that can be cultivated and improved with practice. I must also mention that focus and action go together. Focused action is required to get from the dream, to making the dream a reality. Focus motivates us to take corresponding action in the direction of our goals and dreams.

Remember, you can indeed pursue your dreams and live life on your terms if you are willing set clear goals, and to them move fearlessly in the direction of your dreams. Focus will keep you motivated for your journey to success, and focused action will get you there.

Thank you again for purchasing this book! I hope this book was useful in encouraging you to go after your dreams. The next step is to try the strategies and techniques that you were covered in this book. Choose the ones that work best for you in your quest to achieve your goals.

Finally, if you enjoyed this book, please leave me a positive review. I would greatly appreciate it.

Made in the USA
Monee, IL
08 July 2023